QUESTIONS YOU HAVE ASKED II

Through the Years

EASY BIBLE SURVEY WORKBOOK

#8

Katheryn Maddox Haddad

Other Books by this Author

BIBLICAL HISTORICAL NOVELS
Series of 8: Soul Journey With the Real Jesus
Ongoing Series of 8: Intrepid Men of God

CHILDREN'S BIBLE STORYBOOKS
Series of 8: A Child's Life of Christ
Series of 10: A Child's Bible Heroes
Series of 8: A Child's Bible Kids

WORLDWIDE HISTORICAL RESEARCH
DOCUMENTARY, THESIS, NOVEL & SCREENPLAY WRITERS

BIBLE TOPICS
Applied Christianity: Handbook 500 Good Works
Christianity or Islam? The Contrast
The Holy Spirit: 592 Verses Examined
Inside the Hearts of Bible Women-Reader+Audio+Leader
Revelation: A Love Letter From God
Worship Changes Since 1st Century + Worship 1st Century Way
Was Jesus God? (Why Evil)
365 Life-Changing Scriptures Day by Date
The Road to Heaven
The Lord's Supper: 52 Readings with Prayers

BIBLE FUN BOOKS
Bible Puzzles, Bible Song Book, Bible Numbers

TOUCHING GOD SERIES
365 Golden Bible Thoughts: God's Heart to Yours
365 Pearls of Wisdom: God's Soul to Yours
365 Silver-Winged Prayers: Your Spirit to God's

SURVEY SERIES: EASY BIBLE WORKBOOKS
→Old Testament & New Testament Surveys
→Questions You Have Asked-Part I & II

Genealogy: How to Climb Your Family Tree Without Falling Out
Volume I & 2: Beginner-Intermediate & Colonial-Medieval

ISBN-978-1-952261-51-0
NORTHERN LIGHTS PUBLISHING HOUSE

Contents

Dear Bible Student:

Through the years, people have asked me a variety of honest questions that they have never found a satisfactory answer to.. They are likely to be your questions too. Here is your chance to find out the answers for yourself.

This study book is not to tell you what to believe, but to guide you in your own Bible research to answer your own questions. In every lesson, unless stated otherwise, every verse in the Bible on that topic is listed and considered. If we just pick and choose the verses that lean toward our opinions, we cannot be sure we have God's opinion. It is God who we want to please. Only he has the power to rescue us from hell and share with us his heavenly home.

The NIV (New International Version) Bible is used in this book. All study questions are easy; they just go right down the line, verse by verse. If you meet with a study group, look up your answers at home alone. Remember, your best learning is done when you are studying alone.

May this study book open up new doors of knowledge for you, and new depths of appreciation for our Lord and Savior.

God bless you!

Why Did God Approve Of So Much Violence

Conquerors Not Randomly Selected

GENESIS 15:13-16 – [To Abraham] "Your descendants will be strangers in a country not their own [Egypt], and they will be ____________________ and mistreated ______ years.

"But I will _________________ the nation they serve as slaves, and afterwards they will come out with great ______________________________."

"In the fourth generation [people lived to be about 100 years old then], your descendants will come back _________, for the _____________ of the ___________________________ has not yet reached its ______________ measure."

Conquered Not Randomly Selected

LEVITICUS 18:24-28 - God explained to Moses, after giving the commandments on sexual sins, "Do not ___________________________ yourselves in any of these ways, because this is how the ____________________ I am going to _________________________ before you became defiled. Even the land was defiled; so I _________________ it for its __________________________, and the land _________________________ out its inhabitants....All these things were done by the people who lived in the land ____________ you, and the land became defiled. And if you defile the land, it will vomit ___________________ out as it vomited out the nations that were before you.

DEUTERONOMY 9:5-6 - God did not give the Jews the land of Canaan because they were so good, but because the people before them were so bad. "It is not because of your [Jews'] __________________________________ or your __________________ that you are going in to take possession of ____________________ land; but on account of the _______________ of these _________________, the Lord your God will drive them ___________ before you....for you are a ________________ people.

JOSHUA 24:11-14 just before Joshua died, he recalled to the people how they got their Promised Land from the

A_______________,
P______________________,
C___________________________,
H________________________,
G______________________,
H________________________,
J____________________________

....You did not do it with your own sword and bow. So I gave you a land on which you did ________________ toil and cities you did _____________ build; and you live in them and eat from vineyards and olive groves that you did _________ plant. Now fear the Lord and serve him with ______ faithfulness. Throw away the _____________...and serve the _________________.

Punishers Punished

NOTE: Eventually the Jews did imitate the nations before them, so God vomited them out and they were sent to Babylon.

2 KINGS 21:11 - Manasseh king of Judah has committed these ___________________________ sins. He has done more evil than the _________________ who preceded him and has led Judah into sin with his idols.

2 KINGS 21:6 - He sacrificed his own ___________________ in the _________________ practiced ________________, sought _____________, and consulted ________________ and spiritists. He did much evil in the eyes of the Lord,

arousing his anger.

2 KINGS 21:3b, 5 - He bowed down to all the ____________ ______________________ and worshiped them. ... In the two courts of the ____________________of the Lord, he built ____________________to all the ________________________ ________________________.

2 CHRONICLES 36:15-16 - The Lord, the God of their ancestors, sent word to them through his messengers _____________ and __________________ because he had pity on his people and on his dwelling place. But they __________________ God's messengers, __________________ his words and ___________________ at his prophets until the ___________ of the Lord was aroused against his people and there was no ______________________

2 CHRONICLES 36:20-21 Those who had escaped from the ______________________he carried away to Babylon...until the rule of the kingdom of Persia to _____________________ the word of the Lord by the mouth of __________________ until the land had enjoyed its _________________ [of years]. All the days of its desolation it kept sabbath until ___________________ years were complete.

Love Sometimes Must Resort To Punishment

ROMANS 11:22 - "Consider therefore the ________________ and ___________________ of ____________: Sternness to those who _________________, but kindness to you, ___________________________ that you continue in his ___________________________. Otherwise, you also will be _______________________________.

PROVERBS 3:11-12 - "Do not _____________________ the Lord's _______________________________ and do not __________________ his _________________________, because the Lord disciplines those he _______________, as a father the son he delights in.

2 PETER 3:9 says, "The Lord is not slow in keeping his _________________....He is patient with you, ________ wanting anyone to _________________, but everyone to come to ___________________.

God Sees Things From His Side Of Eternity

Remember when God told Moses he had to die because he struck the rock for water instead of speaking to it? But we know he went to heaven because he appeared centuries later to Jesus (Matthew 17:3). Sometimes God needs to take evil influences out of the way of a new group of people, hoping they will do better.

Undoubtedly good people as well as bad died when Canaan was conquered. But, if they went to heaven, they were much happier then. We must not think of the death of good people as punishment. It is a door to excitement.

What Is Baptism For?

All scriptures below are from the concordance. We will skip the scriptures relating (1) John the Baptist's baptism, (2) baptism of fire, (3) baptism of the Holy Spirit ,and consider only water baptism.

Hebrews 6:2 says as mature Christians, we should "leave the ______________________ teaching" including "instructions about ____________________."

By the time the book of Ephesians was written how many baptisms were there? (See Ephesians 4:5). ____________

Under Heading Of "Baptism"

Romans 6:4 WHAT GOD SAYS: "We were therefore ________________________ with him through ________________________ into death in order that, just as Christ was ________________________ from the dead through the glory of the Father, we too may live a __________ __________________ life."

WHAT THIS VERSE TELLS ME: How do we imitate Jesus' death, burial, and resurrection? ________ ____ _____ ______________________________________

Ephesians 4:5 WHAT GOD SAYS: (See above)

Colossians 2:12 WHAT GOD SAYS: "Having been _______________ with him in ____________________ and _____________________ with him through your faith in the ____ of God, who ________________________ him from the dead."

WHAT THIS VERSE TELLS ME: Can we be buried by having a little dirt or water poured over us? ________

1 Peter 3:21 WHAT GOD SAYS: "And this ____________ symbolizes ______________________________ that now ______________________ you also -- not the removal of dirt from the body but the ________________ of a good ________________________ toward _____________.

WHAT THIS VERSE TELLS ME: What is the final act that saves us? _______________________________

Hebrews 6:2 WHAT GOD SAYS: (See above)

Under Heading Of "To Baptize"

Acts 8:38f WHAT GOD SAYS: "....Then both Philip and the eunuch went ________________________________ the _____________________________________ and Philip _______________________________ him. When they came _______________ ________________ of the water...."

WHAT THIS VERSE TELLS ME: If baptism were pouring, why would Philip have to go down into the water with him? _____________________________
____
____

1 Corinthians 1:14-15 Note that back in verses 11-13 Paul criticized the Christians in Corinth for becoming clannish depending on who baptized them.

WHAT GOD SAYS: "I am thankful that I did not baptize any of you except Crispus and Gaius, so no one can say that you were baptized into __________________ name."

NOTE: Some people use this verse to prove Paul did not like baptism and only did it when forced into it.

WHAT THIS VERSE TELLS ME: We are to be baptized into whose name? ______________________ ____

NOTE: Verse 13 infers they were all baptized. Would Paul have been addressing in whose name they were baptized if they had never been baptized? ____________________

1 Corinthians 1:17 WHAT GOD SAYS: "For Christ did not send me to _________________, but to _______________ the _______________________."

WHAT THIS VERSE TELLS ME: Read 3:6 on the next page regarding Paul's partnership with Apollos. "I [Paul] __________________________ the seed [Word of God], Apollos ___________________________ it, but _________ made it grow. Who apparently did most of the baptizing, following up on Paul's preaching? _________________

Under Heading Of "To Be Baptized"

Mark 16:15-16 WHAT GOD SAYS/ JESUS' ACTUAL WORDS: "He [Jesus] said to them, "Go into all the world and _______________________ the good news to all creation. Whoever ____________________________________ and is _________________________ will be __________________, but whoever does _____________ believe will be condemned.

WHAT THIS VERSE TELLS ME: I will be saved if I do what two things? ___________________________ and ____.

Acts 1:5 Holy Spirit (only spoken to 12 Apostles)

Acts 2:38 WHAT GOD SAYS: "Peter replied, _____________

and be ______________________________ one of you, in the name of Jesus Christ for the _________________ of your _____________. And you will receive the ________________ of the Holy Spirit."

WHAT THIS VERSE TELLS ME: I am to be baptized so what will happen to my sins? ______________

____

Acts 2:41 WHAT GOD SAYS: "Those who ___________ his message were ____________________________, and about ______________________________ were ____________________ to their number that day.

WHAT THIS VERSE TELLS ME: If I accept Peter's message that day, I will do what 3,000 did that day and do what? ____________________________

Acts 8:12f WHAT GOD SAYS: "But when they _______ Philip as he _______________________ the good news of the kingdom of God and the name of Jesus Christ, they were __________________________, both men and women. Simon himself believed and was ____________."

WHAT THIS VERSE TELLS ME: Proof of my belief is exhibited in what act? __________________

Acts 8:16 WHAT GOD SAYS: "....because the Holy Spirit had not yet come upon any of them; they had simply been baptized into the name of the Lord Jesus."

WHAT THIS VERSE TELLS ME: Remember in Mark 16:15, Jesus said people were to baptized in what three names? ____________________________

____

Since the gospel was still new, the Apostles came to give

them the Holy Spirit so as to correct their misunderstanding. Are the Apostles alive today to do this? Therefore, I must be baptized into all three names.

Acts 8:36 WHAT GOD SAYS: "As they traveled along the road, they came to some ________________ and the eunuch said, 'Look, here is ___________________________. Why shouldn't I be baptized?'"

WHAT THIS VERSE TELLS ME: Philip couldn't just pour water from his drinking jug; they had to wait to they came to a body of water to go down into. Therefore, when I am baptized, I cannot have water ______________________ over me to be valid.

Acts 9:17-18 WHAT GOD SAYS: "'...Jesus, who appeared to you on the road as you were coming here - has sent me so that you may see again and be filled with the ____________ _______________.' Immediately, something like scales fell from Saul's eyes, and he could see again. He got up and was ____________________."

WHAT THIS VERSE TELLS ME: I am filled with the Holy Spirit by doing what thing that Saul [the future Apostle Paul] did? ________________________________

Acts 10:47-48 WHAT GOD SAYS: "'Can anyone keep these people from being baptized with _____________? They have received the Holy Spirit just as we have.' So he __________ they be ____________________________ in the name of Jesus Christ."

NOTE: Verse 45 shows that, for the first time, God was accepting Gentiles into his kingdom. The Jews needed a special sign that they were accepted by God, so God gave them the Holy Spirit before their baptism.

WHAT THIS VERSE TELLS ME: If Peter ordered them

to be baptized, how important does this make baptism to me? ____________________________________

Acts 11:16 WHAT GOD SAYS: "'Then I [Peter reporting to the story in Jerusalem] remembered what the Lord had said: 'John baptized with water, but you will be baptized with the Holy Spirit.' So if God gave them the ____________ gift as he gave us...who was I to think that I could _______________ God.'"

WHAT THIS VERSE TELLS ME: Back in Acts 2:38, Peter had told people to receive the gift of the Holy Spirit how? _______________________________. In this incident in Acts 11, he is reflecting the special giving of the gift to the first Gentiles. But ordinarily, according to Acts 2:38, I receive the gift of the Holy Spirit how? ________________________

Acts 16:14b-15 WHAT GOD SAYS: "The Lord opened her heart to _________________________ to Paul's message. When she and the members of her household were _________________________, she invited us to her home."

WHAT THIS VERSE TELLS ME: How am I, today, to respond to Paul's message about Jesus? __________

____

Acts 18:8 WHAT GOD SAYS: "Crispus, the synagogue ruler, and his entire household ______________________ in the Lord; and many of the Corinthians who heard him ____ and were ______________________________."

WHAT THIS VERSE TELLS ME: Can a baby believe?

____

Acts 19:3-6 (Here is another example of early believers not quite understanding what to do and the Apostles (not ordinary Christians) intervening and correcting the situation.

Acts 22:16 WHAT GOD SAYS: "'And now what are you waiting for? _______________ and be ___________________ And _____________________ your ___________ away, calling on his name.'"

WHAT THIS VERSE TELLS ME: Baptism does what to my sins? _________________________________

Romans 6:3) WHAT GOD SAYS: "Or don't you know that ___________ of _____________ who were ________________ into Christ Jesus were ___________________________ into his _________________?"

WHAT THIS VERSE TELLS ME: Through baptism, I imitate what thing that Jesus went through? ____

1 Corinthians 1:13 (See above)

1 Corinthians 10:2 WHAT GOD SAYS: "They [Jews] were all ________________________________ into Moses in the __________________________ and in the sea."

WHAT THIS VERSE TELLS ME: Were the cloud and sea sprinkled onto and under the Jews? Is sprinkling baptism? ________________________

1 Corinthians 12:13 WHAT GOD SAYS: "For we were ____ by one Spirit ______________ one ___________________...and we were ___________ given the one ______________________ to drink."

WHAT THIS VERSE TELLS ME: Ephesians 1:22-23 says the body is the church. Therefore, when I am baptized, I am baptized into what? _________________

1 Corinthians 15:29 WHAT GOD SAYS: "Now if there is no _______________________________, what will those do who

are ________________ for the dead? If the dead are not raised at all, why are people ________________________ for them?"

WHAT THIS VERSE TELLS ME: Remember Romans 6 says we are baptized into the ______________ of Jesus in hope that some day we will be _______________________ with him to live eternally. Do I want to be raised with Jesus in baptism now so I can be raised with him eternally? ________________

Galatians 3:27 WHAT GOD SAYS: "For ________________ of you who were ___________________ into Christ have clothed yourselves with ________________________."

WHAT THIS VERSE TELLS ME: When I am baptized, I put on who? _________________________

Under Heading "Baptzing"

Matthew 28:19 WHAT GOD SAYS, AND JESUS' ACTUAL WORDS: "Therefore, go and make _________of all nations, _________________________ them in the name of the ___________________________________, and of the ____________________________________ and of the _________________________, and teaching them to obey ____ I have ___________________________ you."

WHAT THIS VERSE TELLS ME: Baptism is one of Jesus' commands. If I am to at least try to obey every one of his commands, what will I do? _____________

SCRIPTURE	PEOPLE	HEARD	BELIEVED	REPENTED	CONFESSED	BAPTIZED	PRAYED SINNER'S PRAYER
Acts 2: 37-41, 47	3000 Jews* Jerusalem	x	x	x		x	
Acts 8: 5-6, 12	People in Samaria	x	x			x	
Acts 8: 30-39	Ethiopian	x			x	x	
Acts 9 3-6, 17-19	Saul/Paul** (future apostle)	x				x	
Acts 10: 1-2. 48	Cornelius & Household*					x	
Acts 16: 14-15	Lydia & Household	x				x	
Acts 18: 1, 8	Corinthians		x			x	
Acts 19: 1-6	Ephesians		x			x	
Acts 22: 7-16	Saul/Paul** (future apostle)	x				x	

**Receiving Holy Spirit is another study. Notice, even though he was morally upright, he still had to do something else.*
***Notice, even though he had seen a vision of Jesus, he still had to do something else.*

Now back off from this page for a moment and look at the chart without being able to read what it says. Something stands out. It is the fact that only one row is completely checked off. What is that row? Some things were taken for granted, but the writers always emphasized one thing so that people would never take it for granted. They were all baptized! Isn't that amazing?

My Relative Died Without Being Baptized,
But Was The Most Godly Person I Knew

God knows whether your loved one would have been baptized had they known about it. Do you want people who look up to you to use you as their excuse not to be baptized? Someone in your family must break the cycles. Be that someone.

What Is The Unforgivable Sin?

Luke 12:10 - "And everyone who speaks a word against the Son of Man will be forgiven, but anyone who blasphemes against the Holy Spirit will not be forgiven."

John 14:16-17a - "I will ask the Father and he will give you another ___________________ to be with you forever - the Spirit of ________________.

John 17:17 - "Sanctify them by the truth. Your ______________ is truth."

Since the Holy Spirit is the truth and the truth is the word of God, then people who do not believe the word of God cannot be forgiven.

Should I Have My Baby Baptized?

The reasoning given by church leaders for baptizing infants is that it is a Christian substitute for Jewish circumcision.

To be consistent, babies must be baptized on the eighth day and can only be boys. And, everyone who works for that family must also have their baby boys circumcised or be fired. (See Genesis 17:12,13).

The only time baptism is mentioned in connection with circumcision is this [capitals mine]:

"In him you were also circumcised, in the putting off of the sinful nature, NOT with a circumcision done BY THE HANDS OF MEN but with the circumcision done by Christ, having been BURIED WITH HIM IN BAPTISM and raised with him through YOUR FAITH in the power of God, who raised him from the dead.

"When you were dead in your sins and in the uncircumcision of your sinful nature, God made you alive with Christ. He forgave us all our sins, having canceled the written code [Old Testament] with its regulations, that was against us and that stood opposed to us; he took it away, nailing it to the cross" (Colossians 2:11-14). This scripture refers to someone with faith and a form of circumcision not performed by men, which would eliminate babies and baptism which is performed by men.

Further, whenever the apostles argued with Jewish Christians not to circumcise their babies as a religious rite, never did he tell them to baptize their babies instead (Acts 15:1-21; 1 Corinthians 7:17-20; Galatians 2:3-5; 5:1-12; 6:1216).

Never in the scriptures is there a story saying directly that a baby was baptized. None. Preachers who practice this

will say it is inferred when entire households were baptized. But if you investigate these, you will find those entire households also believed. Can infants believe?

The scripture most cited for infant baptism is in the Old Testament where David said in Psalm 51:5, "Surely I was sinful at birth, sinful from the time my mother conceived me."

David had just had to admit he had committed adultery and she was now pregnant. It nearly killed him. And while he was at it, he referred to the adulterous situation under which his lineage was born, as though "It has happened again."

Why? Because Deuteronomy 23:2, part of the Law of Moses David lived under, says, "No one born of a forbidden marriage nor any of his descendants may enter the assembly of the Lord, even down to the tenth generation." What was a forbidden marriage? Among others, it was one between a father and daughter-in-law (Leviticus 18:15).

Genesis 38 says that Judah's son married Tamar and then died. But for various reasons, his brothers refused to carry on their deceased brother's name as commanded in Deuteronomy 24:5-10. So she dressed up like a prostitute, and when Judah, newly widowed, saw her, he went to bed with her. As a result, she had an illegitimate son named Perez, David's ancestor.

Matthew 1:3-6 gives the lineage of David. Counting the generations between Perez and David reveals it to be ten generations (remember Deuteronomy 23:2 regarding this?). In this sense, David was conceived in sin. (And, by the way, it was his son, Solomon of the 11th generation who built the temple.)

All babies and little children are as saved as adult

Christians. Hebrews 1:14 says, "Are not all angels ministering spirits sent to serve those who will inherit salvation?" And Jesus himself said in Matthew 18:10, "'See that you do not look down on one of these little ones. For I tell you that their angels in heaven always see the face of my Father in heaven.'" Did he say only baptized children? Never.

Further, Jesus said in Matthew 19:14, "Let the little children come to me, and do not hinder them, for the kingdom of heaven belongs to such as these." He did not say, for the kingdom of heaven belongs to children after they are baptized. He said the kingdom of heaven right now belongs to them.

Never did David believe a baby was doomed to hell. This psalm was written when he found out Bathsheba was pregnant by him outside of wedlock. The account of that event is in 2 Samuel 11 and 12. After the baby was born, he got sick and died seven days later, too early to be scriptural circumcised. Did David believe his uncircumcised baby went to hell? No. He said, "'Can I bring him back again? I will go to him, but he will not return to me'" (2 Samuel 12:23).

Do We Have Guardian Angels?

Psalm 34:7 The ____________________of the Lord encamps around those who ____________________ him, and he delivers them.

Matthew 18:10 See that you do not __________________ one of these __________________ ones. For I tell you that their _________________ in heaven always see the _________________of my Father in heaven.

Hebrews 1:14 Are not all ____________________ministering spirits sent to __________________those who will ____________________salvation?

Tongues /Languages

In the original Greek language of the New Testament, the word is "GLOSSA"

Below are all scriptures listed in the Bible Concordance using the word ***glossa*** regardless of English Translation.

Mark 16:15ff "Go into all the ___________________ and preach the good news to all creation....And these signs will accompany [Greek is follow] those who believe: In my name they will drive out demons; they will speak in new ___________________________; they will pick up snakes with their hands; and when they drink deadly poison, it will not hurt them at all; they will place their hands on sick people, and they will get well."

> Did each individual new Christians receive all these gifts (1 Corinthians 12:7-11)? _________________
>
> If the gift of tongues still exists today, why aren't certain Christians able to pick up poisonous snakes and drink poison without getting sick and/or dying?
>
> ____
>
> The word translated "new" is from the Greek ***kainos*** meaning new. The word for unknown is the Greek ***agnoeo*** or ***agnostos*** (hence agnostic who doesn't know if there is a God). This word is used only three times in the New Testament, and never regarding languages. (See Acts 17:23, 2 Corinthians 6:9, Galatians 1:22).

Acts 2:4 "All of them were filled with the Holy Spirit and began to speak in other _______________________ as the Spirit enabled them."

What does the footnote say the word tongues means?

____

The word translated "other" is from the Greek ***heteros*** meaning different; it never means unknown.

Who Received This Gift?

1:15 How many were present when they selected a replacement for Judas? __________________

2:1 Was Pentecost on the same day? _______________

Who were the "they" referred to as being present that day (check v. 3, 4, 7, 14, 15)? ____________________________

Acts 2:7 & 11 "Are not all these _______________ who are __________________ Galileans? ....we hear them declaring the wonders of God in our ____________________ tongues!"

What does the footnote say the other translation of the word tongues is? __________________________

Did these people hear only Peter speak? __________

Who did they hear speak?_______________________
____

Could it possibly have been that each apostle spoke in the language of one of the groups of people, but only Peter's sermon was recorded?

2:14 How many were present when Pentecost came who got the gift? __________ Therefore, how many received this gift to speak in tongues? __________

2:9 How many regions were represented that day (count them below)? ________________________

REGION	AREA	An Apostle Sent Them a Letter Written in Greek
Parthia	Mideast	
Media	Mideast	
Elam	Mideast	
Mesopotamia	Mideast	
Judea	Mideast	Matthew
Cappadocia	Turkey	Peter
Pontus	Turkey	Peter
Asia	Turkey	Ephesus, Colossae,
Phrygia	Turkey	
Pamphylia	Turkey	
Egypt	Africa	
Libya	Africa	
Rome	Italy	Romans
Crete	Turkey	Titus
Arabia	Mideast	

At least five of these regions spoke Greek because letters were sent to them by the Apostles written in Greek. Therefore, not all the regions represented spoke languages different from the others.

2:37 "When the people heard this, they were cut to the heart and said to Peter and the ________________________
____
____."

Was Peter the only one who spoke to the people that day? ___________________

2:6 Who did the people hear so that they were hearing in their own languages? _____________________________

Acts 10:45f "The circumcised believers who had come with Peter were astonished that the gifts of the Holy Spirit had been poured out ________________________________ on ____. For they _________________________________ them speaking in _______________________________ and praising God.

The word translated "heard" is from the Greek ***akouo*** which means to harken with understanding, a form of communication. The same word is used to indicate the fellowship between Jesus and Jehovah (John 8:26, 40) and between Paul and Timothy (2 Timothy 2:2).

If everyone present heard the Gentiles, understanding their communication, was it in an unknown language? _____________________________

If everyone present heard and believed, were there any babies present? ______________________________

Acts 19:6 "When Paul placed his hands on them, the Holy Spirit came on them, and they _______________ in tongues and prophesied."

The word translated "spoke" is from the Greek ***laleo*** meaning to tell something or converse.

Romans 3:13-14 "Their throats are open graves; their tongues practice _______________________________." "The poison of vipers is on their lips." "Their mouths are full of cursing and bitterness."

Would someone using a gift of tongues be lying and cursing so as to offend others? _____________ This word "tongue" is the same word as in all the others above.

Philippians 2:11 "...and every tongue ________________ that Jesus Christ is Lord, to the glory of God the Father."

The word translated "confess" is from the Greek

exomologeo which is a public acknowledgment, something done openly among others.

Would the public know what was being confessed and known if an unknown language was being used to do so? ______________ ________________________

James 1:26 "If anyone considers himself __________________ and yet does not keep a tight ______________________ on his ___________________________, he ___________________ himself and his religion is _________________________."

If we use our tongue improperly, what happens to all the religion we are practicing? _____________________

____

James 3:5 "Likewise the tongue is a small part of the body, but it makes great ___________________________. Consider what a great forest is set on fire by a small spark."

If we are boasting in an unknown language, how could anyone else know we were boasting? ___________

James 3:6 "The tongue also is a fire, a world of __________________ among the parts of the body. It corrupts the whole person, sets the whole course of his life on fire, and is itself set on fire by hell."

Left unbridled, the tongue can influence the world, though tiny. And it can change the course of someone's life. If this were an unknown language, how could it possibly hurt anyone else? __________________

James 3:8 "But no man can tame the tongue. It is a ____ full of ________________________________ poison."

Since the tongue cannot be tamed, it must be bridled (see context). But, once again, could it do any harm at all if this were an unknown language? _______________ 1 Peter 3:8ff "...live in ______________________ with one another; be ___________________________, love as brothers, be ____ and humble. Do not repay evil with evil or _________________, because to this you were called so that you may inherit a blessing. For "whoever would ____________________________ life and see ___________________________ days must keep his tongue from ___________________ and his lips from ______________ speech."

Could our Christian family know we were insulting or blessing if we were speaking in an unknown language?

1 John 3:18 "Dear children, let us not love with __________ or __________________________ but with actions and in _________________________________."

In context, John is saying our religion should not be just talk. Could others be able to tell whether we were hypocrites if we were speaking in an unknown tongue?

The word translated "word" here comes from the Greek word "logos" meaning logic and reason.

Would an unknown tongue be observed by others to be with logic and reason? ______________________

Babble

Matthew 6:7 "And when you ______________________, do not keep on babbling like _________________________, for they think they will be heard because of their ___________________ words."

The word translated "babble" is from the Greek ***batto-***

logeo meaning to speak emptily. ("Logos" means

expressed logic.)

Acts 17:18 "A group of...philosophers began to dispute with him. Some of them asked, 'What is this babbler trying to _____________________? He seems to be advocating foreign gods.' They said this because Paul was preaching the good news about Jesus and the ___________________________."

The word translated "babble" in this case is from the Greek "sperm-a-logos," meaning to speak words picked up like scraps of food with no real meat to them. ("Logos" means expressed logic.)

These people understood Paul's words. They were insulting him because they disagreed with him.

1 Timothy 6:20 "Timothy, guard what has been entrusted to your care. Turn away from godless _________________ and the opposing ideas of what is falsely called ___________ ______________________, which some have professed and in so doing have ______________________________________ from the ______________________."

The word translated "chatter" is from the Greek word ***keno-phonia*** which means empty sounds. The KJV translated "godless chatter" to "vain babblings."

2 Timothy 2:16 "Avoid godless chatter, because those who ___________________________ in it will become more and more ____________________________________."

Same Greek word as above - sounds empty of meaning.

Groanings

Romans 8:26 In the same way, the Spirit helps us in our weakness. We do not know what we ought to pray for, but the

Spirit himself intercedes for us with______________________ that words cannot express.

The word translated "groans" in the Greek is ***stenagmos*** which means to sigh. This word appears only one other time in the Bible:

Acts 7:34 "...my people in Egypt. have heard their groaning...."

Were they speaking in an unknown language? ____________

1st Corinthians
Why Was It Written?

1:10,11 Some people from Chloe's household had reported to Paul that the church in Corinth was having _______________________________ among each other.

3:1 They were acting like ________________________.

3:3 They were still ____________________________.

4:6 One man was taking ____________________________ over another.

4:14 & 18 Paul had to write to ______________________ them as children because some had become ________________.

5:6 They were also _________________________, which was not good.

5:8 Their lives were still full of the yeast of ______________ and ________________.

6:12 Although things they were doing might be permissible, they were being ____________________ by them.

7:26 They were in the middle of a c_____________________.

10:24 They were seeking their own ___________________ and not the good of __________________.

11:17 Their MEETINGS were doing more ______________ than __________________________.

14:36 Some of them were acting like the word of God had ____________________________ with them.

2 Corinthians 2:1 In order to avoid making another __________ visit to them.

2:4 Paul was greatly __________________________ and _____________________________ in heart, and had shed many __________________________ over them.

This Letter was a Reply to Their Letter

1 Corinthians 1:11 Possibly written and delivered by Chloe's household, or maybe they went to see Paul in addition to the letter someone else sent about all their quarrels.

7:1 "Now for the matters you wrote about."

His Reply to Their Letter Divided Into Two Parts

Ch. 7-11a Their Private Christian Lives

7:1ff MARRIAGE: "It is good for a man not to marry...."

8:1ff IDOLATROUS MEALS: "Now about

food sacrificed to idols...."

9:1-3 PAYMENT OF PREACHERS: "This is my defense to those who sit in judgment on me...."

10:1ff IDOLATROUS MEALS: Continuation of above

11:1-16 PRAYING AND PROPHESYING TO HUSBAND OR WIFE AT HOME

Ch. 11b-16 Their Christian Assembly

11:17-34 KEEPING THE LORD'S SUPPER IN ASSEMBLY: "In the FOLLOWING" directives...your MEETINGS...."

12:1-31 SPIRITUAL GIFTS USED IN ASSEMBLY: "....Message of wisdom...message of knowledge ...healing...prophecy... tongues..interpretation ..." etc. (12:8-10).

13:1-13 LOVE'S SUPERIORITY TO TONGUES

14:1-25 TONGUES IN THE ASSEMBLY

14:26-40 ORDERLINESS IN ASSEMBLY

15:1-58 WHAT THEY MUST PREACH RE. RESURRECTION OF DEAD: "But if it is preached....how can some of you say that there is no resurrection of the dead?" (15:12).

16:1-4 COLLECTIONS IN ASSEMBLY: "Now about the collection...."

All Mention Of Tongues In 1 Corinthians 12 & 13

12:10 ....to another miraculous powers, to another prophecy, to another distinguishing between spirits, to another speaking in ____of tongues....

The word translated "kinds of" is from the Greek word "genos" which means race, nationality.

12:10 ....and to still another the ____________________ ____________________ of tongues.

The word translated "interpretation" in Greek is **hermeneia** which is an explanation, a commentary.

12:28 And in the church, God has appointed first of all ______________________________, second prophets, third teachers, then workers of miracles, also those having gifts of healing, those able to help others, those with gifts of administration, and those speaking in ________________ kinds of tongues.

The word translated "first of all" in Greek is "proton" which means order in rank or order of importance.

What was put last in this list of importance? __________________________________

If the gift of tongues exists today, what else in this list must of necessity also exist? ______________________
____
____

The word translated "different kinds" in Greek is ***genos*** indicating race or nationality.

12:30 Do all have gifts of healing? Do all ________________ ________________________ in tongues? Do all interpret?

The word translated "speak" in Greek is ***laleo*** which means to tell something.

Can we tell something to someone else if we are speaking in an unknown language?

13:1 If I speak in the ______________________________ of men and of ____________________________, but have not love, I am only a resounding ______________________ or a ________________________________ cymbal.

If you have a King James Version of the Bible, note that the word "unknown" is italicized. That means that this word is not in the original Greek.

So, What Language Do Angels Speak In?

To find out, complete the chart below, telling what language these people understood. Do you see any similarity between the tongues of angels and the tongues spoken by the apostles and heard by the different nationalities on Pentecost in Acts 2?

13:8 Love never fails. But where there are prophecies, they will cease; where there are tongues, they will be ___________________________________.

The word translated "be stilled" is ***pauomai*** which means to stop, to make an end. In Luke 8:24, for instance, this word is used for the storm ceasing.

In the chart below fill in what language they spoke in.

SCRIPTURE	PERSON THE ANGEL APPEARED TO	SCRIPTURE	LANGUAGE THE PERSON & ANGEL SPOKE IN

Genesis 16:7-12	Hagar	Genesis 16:3	
Genesis 19:10-21	Lot's Family	Genesis 11:31	
Genesis 21:14-18	Hagar	Genesis 16:3	
Genesis 22:1-12	Abraham	Genesis 11:31	
Exodus 3:1-3	Moses	Exodus 1:15, 2:9-10	
Judges 13:2-17	Samson's Parents	Judges 13:1	
2 Kings 1:3-4	Elijah	1 Kings 17:1	
Daniel 8:16-25; 9:21-27	Daniel	Daniel 1:1-4	
Luke 1:8-20	Zechariah, John's Father	Luke 1:4	
Luke 1:28-38	Mary	Luke 3:24-25 (Mary's genealogy)	
Luke 2:8-12	Shepherds	Luke 2:4	
Matthew 28:1-7	Mary Magdalene & others		Magdala, Galilee in Palestine
Acts 10:1-8	Cornelius	Acts 10:1	
Acts 12:5-10	Peter	John 1:44	
Revelation 5:2, etc., etc.	John	Matthew 4:18-21	

The next page begins a verse-by-verse study of 1 Corinthians 14. Note the context in which he writes the chapter (although remember that chapter breaks were added 14 centuries later):

11:17 ...for your meetings do....
11:33 ...when you come together....
12:28 ...in the church, God has appointed....
14:6 ...if I come to you (plural) and speak....
14:23 ...So if the whole church comes together....
14:26 ....When you come together....
14:33 ....As in all the congregations....
15:12 ....But if it is preached....
16:1 ....Now about the collection....

13:1 & 13 And now I will show you the _______________ excellent way....But the greatest of these is _____________.

1 Corinthians14

14:1 Follow the way of love and eagerly __________ ________________________________ spiritual gifts, ____________________________.

The word translated "prophecy" is from the Greek word ***prophateau*** and means to publicly expound on a subject (not necessarily tell the future).

If we want to lovingly help other people the most, what will we prefer above all spiritual gifts? ____________ ________________________________

12:7-10 Look back at this list. Note that the first two gifts listed involve messages. What was the last gift listed? _____________

12:28-30 Remember this list was given in order of importance? What were the first two in the list? ____ _ ________________________ What were the last two? ____________________________________ ______________________

Yet, Paul had to dedicate an entire chapter (14) to tongues because they were not only misusing it, but they were preferring and magnifying it above the others.

14:2 For anyone who __________________________ in a tongue does not speak to men but to God. Indeed, no one _____________________________ him; he utters __________________________ with his spirit.

What is the context for chapters 11 through 16?

Private behavior or public worship? ________________

Note the footnote giving a translation of tongue. What is it? ____________________________________

Would the congregation in Corinth likely to be able to understand Persian or Egyptian or etc.? ________

14:3 But ____ who ______________________________________ speaks to men for their strengthening, encouragement and comfort.

Once more, Paul is talking about the assembly of the church where? _________________________________

A prophet without the gift of languages would have no choice but to speak in his own language. Obviously, then, the people hearing him would be able to what?

____

14:4 He who speaks in a tongue edifies ____________________, but he who prophesies edifies the ______________________________________

Considering verses 2 and 3, why would this be? ____

14:5 I would like ___________________ of you to speak in tongues, but I would ___________________________ you prophesy. He who prophesies is __________________________ than the one who speaks in __________________________ _______________, unless he ______________________ so that the church may be edified.

You can test people who speak in tongues. Ask them to record them doing so. Then play the recording to them and other people who claim the gift of interpretation, but all separately, and see if they all give the same interpretation.

14:6 Now, brothers, if I come to you and speak in tongues, what good will I be to you, unless I bring you some ______________________________ or ______________________________ or ______________________________ or word of ______________________________?

> Tongues must include the above. If you hear an interpretation of tongues and it is exclusively praises to God, for instance, that is wrong.
>
> Remember, these things were necessary before the entire New Testament was written out. People did not always know what to do in various situations. But by the time Revelation was written, God said through John:
>
> Revelation 22:18-19 I ______________________ everyone who hears the words of the prophecy of this ______________________: If anyone __________ anything to them, God will add to him the plagues described in this book. And if anyone takes words ______________________ from this book of prophecy, God will take away from him his share in the tree of life and in the holy city, which are described in this book.

14:7 Even in the case of ______________________ things that make ______________________, such as the flute or harp, how will anyone ______________________ what tune is

being played unless there is a ______________________ in the notes?

> Could this verse possibly mean "Even in the case of living people that make words, such as men and women, how will anyone know what message is being said unless there is a distinction in the words?"

____

If this is not the meaning, what could it be? __________
____

14:8 Again, if the trumpet does not sound a ____________ ______________________________, who will get ready for the ______________________________?

If a trumpet is played for a battle or taps or reveille, how will the army know how to respond to the trumpet?

14:9 So it is with you. ______________________________ you speak ____ words with your tongue, ________________________________ will anyone ______________________________ what you are saying? You will just be speaking into the __________________________.

How much clearer can Paul be? Their words must be _________________________ or they must stay quiet.

14:10 Undoubtedly there are all sorts of _________________ in the world, yet _________________ of them is without ____________________________________.

Did he say languages in the world or languages in a spiritual realm? ________________________________

14:11 If then I do not __________________________ the _________________________________ of what someone is saying, I am a __________________________________ to the speaker, and he is a foreigner to me.

Did Paul say that if I don't grasp, I'm not as spiritual as the speaker? ______________________ Did he mean that if I don't grasp, I'm a sinner and the speaker is a Christian? ______________________ Did he say that I don't grasp that particular nation's language? ________

14:12 So it is with you. Since you are eager to have spiritual gifts, try to excel in gifts that ______________________________ the ____________________________________.

> If I'm speaking in a language in the church that no one understands, am I edifying the church? ___________________
>
> Am I, then, defying what Paul told us to do here? __________

14:13 For this reason anyone who speaks in a tongue should pray that he may ______________________________ what he says.

> The word translated "interpret" is from the Greek word ***diermeneuo*** which is an intense use of the word ***hermeneuo*** which means to THOROUGHLY explain. This same word is used in describing what Jesus did on the road to Emmaus:
>
> Luke 24:27 - And beginning with Moses and all the Prophets, he ______________________________ to them what was said in all the Scriptures concerning himself.
>
> Although the book of Nehemiah was written in Hebrew, the same thing happened when Ezra read the Law of Moses for the first time to the Jews after they were freed from Babylonian captivity:
>
> Nehemiah 8:8 - They read from the Book of the Law of God, making it ______________________________ and giving the ____________________________________ so that the people could ____________________________ what was being read.
>
> FURTHER, this word was used in the following verses to interpret the word from one language to another:
>
> John 1:38 - They said, "Rabbi" (which means Teacher),

"where are you staying?"

Acts 9:36 - In Joppa there was a disciple named Tabitha (which, when translated, is Dorcas).

In either case above, was there a word translated from an unknown tongue to a known language?

14:14 For if I pray in a tongue, my spirit prays, but my ________________________________ is unfruitful [doesn't change my life].

The word translated "mind" is from the Greek word ***nous*** meaning "understanding" and is translated as such in the KJV and other versions. It is also used in the following scriptures:

Luke 24:45 - Then he [Jesus] OPENED their minds so they could UNDERSTAND the scriptures.

Romans 1:28 - Since they did not think it worthwhile to retain the KNOWLEDGE of God....

Romans 14:5 - Each one should be fully CONVINCED in his own mind.

Revelation 13:18 - This calls for wisdom. If anyone has INSIGHT, let him calculate....

Have you ever read a scripture and not known what it means?

The word translated "unfruitful" is from the Greek word ***akarpos*** and is used in the following verses:

Matthew 13:22 - What choked out the Word of God from these hearts? ________________________
____

Ephesians 5:3-4, 11 - What kinds of things put us in darkness away from God? ______________________
____

What puts us into the light (Eph. 5:10)? ____________
____

Titus 3:14 - We live unfruitful lives if we do not do what?
____

2 Peter 1:5-8 - "For if you possess these qualities in increasing measure, they will keep you from being
____
and _____________________________________ in your _____________________________________
[what some got from those who spoke in tongues] of our Lord Jesus Christ.

Jude 10, 12 - "These men speak abusively against whatever they do not _____________________
....They are clouds without rain, blown along by the wind; autumn trees, without fruit and uprooted - twice
__________________________."

IN A NUTSHELL, if someone has the word of God but is unfruitful, they do not know how to apply the word of God to their lives - interpret the scriptures.

14:15 So what shall I do? I will _____________________ [aloud - this is a public worship assembly] with my spirit, but I will also pray with my _______________________________ [understanding]; I will sing with my spirit, but I will also _____________________________ with my mind.

Just as we sing using words we understand, we must also pray using words we understand.

14:16 "If you are praising God with your spirit, how can one who finds himself __________________________ those who do not ______________________________ say "Amen" to your thanksgiving, since he does not ______________________________ what you are saying?

Are we then told to say "Amen" to the prayers of those praying aloud in our assembly? __________ Can we say "Amen" to unintelligible words? __________

14:17 You may be giving thanks well enough, _____ the other man is ______________________________ ______________________________.

Do unintelligible words of someone else edify you? ________

14:18 I thank God that I speak in tongues ______________ than all of you.

Paul was a great missionary and traveled to many parts of the world preaching. So had the other apostles, for Jesus told them in Mark 16:15-16 to "Go into all the world and preach the gospel." How effective had it been?

Acts 17:6 "These men who have caused trouble all over the ____________________ have now come here.

Romans 1:8 "...your faith is being reported all over the ______________________."

Romans 10:18 "Their voice has gone out into all the ______________________, their words to the ends of the ______________________."

Colossians 1:23 "This is the gospel that you heard and that has been proclaimed to ________________ creature under ______________________, and of which I, Paul, have become a servant.

According to secular history....

Andrew went to Greece	Europe
Peter went to Turkey, Greece, & Italy	Europe
Thaddeus went to Russia	Europe
Thomas went to India	Asia
Philip went to Turkey	Europe
Nathaniel went to Russia	Europe
Matthew went to Ethiopia and Egypt	Africa
Simon went to Great Britain	Europe

14:19 But in the ________________________________ I would rather speak five ______________________ words to ____________ others than __________________________ ______________________ words in a tongue.

14:20 Brothers, stop thinking like ______________________ ______________________. In regard to evil be infants, but in your _______________________________________ be _________________________.

Their showing off their ability to speak in a foreign language in their home congregation was considered by Paul to be what? ____________________________

14:21 [Isaiah 28:11-12] In the Law it is written: "Through men of ______________________ tongues and through the lips of ________________ I will speak to this people, but even then they will not listen to me," says the Lord.

This is a prophecy to the Jews that some day God will send messengers to them from among foreigners. Do you think they could have gotten their message across if they were speaking unintelligible words? _________

14:22 Tongues, then, are a __________________, not for

believers but for ______________________________; prophecy, however, is for believers, not for unbelievers.

The gift of tongues was used to give the initial gospel message, and used by missionaries. The gift of prophecy was used by some of the members so they could know God's will for their lives before the written New Testament existed.

14:23 So if the whole ______________________________ comes together and everyone speaks in tongues, and [a] some who do not ______________________________ or [b] some ______________________ come in, will they not say that you are ____ ______?

How can Paul be any clearer?

14:24-25 But if an ______________________________________ or someone who does not ______________________________ [footnote indicates "inquirer"] comes in while everybody is ____, he will be ____ by all that he is a ____ and will be judged by all, and the secrets of his heart will be laid bare. So he will fall down and worship God exclaiming, "____ __________________________."

Do our church services center around serving only the members with no thought for visitors who are searching for truth and/or relief of pain in their lives?

14:26 What then shall we say, brothers? When you ____ everyone has a hymn, or a word of instruction, a revelation, a tongue or an interpretation. All of these must be done for the ____ of the __________________________.

If I do not understand someone's unintelligible words, they may be having a good time, but am I learning anything, according to Paul? ______________________

14:27 If anyone speaks in a tongue, two - or at the most three - should speak, one at a time, and someone ________________________ interpret.

Every time someone speaks in a tongue, they must pause and wait for someone to interpret before the next one can do it. (Even though he still thinks it is showing off.)

14:28 If there is no ____________________________, the speaker should keep ____________________ in the ______________________________ and speak to himself and God.

Perhaps this person should get back on the circuit and spread the gospel if he/she wants to speak in that foreign language so much.

14:29 Two or three ____________________________ should speak, and the others [other prophets - see v. 32] should ___________ carefully what is said.

14:30 And if a ______________________________ comes to someone who is sitting down, the first speaker should stop.

14:31 For you can all prophesy in turn so that everyone may be ____ and ____.

Does speaking in a foreign language or unintelligible words instruct and encourage us?

14:32 The spirits of prophets are subject to the _________________________ of prophets.

Why Am I Not Spiritual Enough To Be Slain In The Spirit?

The phrase, "slay in the Spirit" is no where in the Bible.

Examples of those upon whom the Spirit came and shifted their position never fell down, but always stood up:

Ezekiel 2:2 - "As he spoke, the Spirit came into me and ________ me to my __________."

Ezekiel 3:24 - "Then the Spirit came into me and ___________ me to my ____________.

Why Don't Healing Services Cure Me?

Who Has Miraculous Powers

Once again, there are too many scriptures with the word "healing" or "miracle" in it, so the following is a summary study. If interested in more, look up all the scriptures in a concordance.

Exodus 20:22; 21:1 - Who introduced the era of Old Testament Law? ________________

Exodus 7-10; 14:21 - Give some examples of his miracles to prove he was from God. ____________
____
____

Deuteronomy 34:9 - On whom did Moses transfer his miraculous powers?
____

Joshua never passed miraculous powers on to anyone else.

1 Kings 17:1 - Who introduced the era of prophets?
____

1 Kings 17:12-15; 18-22; 18:34-38 - Give some examples of his miracles to prove he was from God.
____
____
____

2 Kings 2:9-11 - On whom did Elijah transfer his miraculous powers? _________________________

Elisha never passed miraculous powers on to anyone else.

Acts 1:4, 8, 2:38; 41-43 - Who introduced the era of Christianity? ______________________________

Acts 3:6-8; 9:40; 20:9-10 - Give some examples of their miracles to prove they were from God.__________
____
____
____

Acts 6:5-6; 8; 8:6 - On whom did the apostles transfer their miraculous powers? ____________________

Romans 1:1,11 - What title did Paul hold? __________
Why did he want to visit the church in Rome?___ ____________________________
____

If they could just pray for those gifts, why would his long trip be necessary?

1 Corinthians 1:6-7 - To whom did Paul impart spiritual gifts?
__________________________________.

1 Corinthians 11:17 - Did having these spiritual gifts necessarily make them better or superior Christians?

____

2 Corinthians 12:12 - What were the signs that marked an apostle? ________________________________

Day Of Pentecost

Below is a verse-by-verse look at Acts 2:16-21 (a quotation of Joel 2:28-32).

Acts 2:16-17a - "This is what was spoken by the prophet Joel: 'In the LAST DAYS, God says I will pour out my Spirit on ALL people....'"

I Peter 1:19-20 says the latter days began when?

____

Acts 2:17b - "....Your sons and daughters will PROPHESY...."

Luke 1:5, 67 - What descendant (son) of Aaron prophesied about Jesus? ______________________

Luke 2:25-35 - What other "son" of the Israelites prophesied about Jesus? _____________________

Luke 1:5, 41-45 - What descendant (daughter) of Aaron prophesied about Jesus? ____________________

Luke 2:36-38 - What other "daughter" of the Israelites prophesied about Jesus? ____________________

Acts 2:17c - "....Your young men will see visions, your old men will dream dreams. Even on my servants, both men and women, I will pour out my Spirit in those days, and they will prophesy...."

Matthew 1:20-23 - What young man dreamed a dream? ______________________ [Don't be fooled by that old tradition that he was an old man. He was still alive when Jesus preached (notice present tense in John 6:42).]

Matthew 2:1, 12 - What old men dreamed a dream?

____

Luke 1:11f, 22 - What old man saw a vision? _________

Luke 2:25-35 - What other "son" of the Israelites prophesied about Jesus? _____________________

Luke 1:5, 41-45 - What descendant (daughter) of Aaron

prophesied about Jesus? ____________________

Luke 2:36-38 - What other "daughter" of the Israelites prophesied about Jesus? ____________________

Acts 2:17c - "....Your young men will see visions, your old men will dream dreams. Even on my servants, both men and women, I will pour out my Spirit in those days, and they will prophesy...."

Matthew 1:20-23 - What young man dreamed a dream? ______________________ [Don't be fooled by that old tradition that he was an old man. He was still alive when Jesus preached (notice present tense in John 6:42).]

Matthew 2:1, 12 - What old men dreamed a dream?

____

Luke 1:11-12, 22 - What old man saw a vision?

____

Acts 1:9 - ___________________________________

Acts 2:2 - ___________________________________

Acts 2:19b - "....and SIGNS on the earth below...."

Below, list the signs on earth that occurred:

Luke 2:12 - ____________________________
Matthew 12:39-40 - _____________________
Luke 2:34 - ___________________________
John 4:48 - ___________________________
John 2:18-28 - _________________________

John 20:30f - Who performed many miraculous signs and why? _________________________

Acts 2:22 - How did God give accreditation to Jesus among the people on earth? ______________________

____

Acts 2:19c - "....BLOOD and FIRE and BILLOWS of smoke...."

Acts 2:23 - Whose blood were the prophet and Peter referring to? ______________________

Acts 2:3 - What fire were the prophet and Peter referring to? ______________________

Acts 2:2 - What billows of smoke were the prophet and Peter referring to? ______________________

This phrase, "billows of smoke" could also be translated "breath of God's glory." "Breath" is also translated "wind."

Exodus 19:9 - Who came in a cloud to Mt. Sinai? ______________________

2 Chronicles 7:1-3 - What of the Lord filled the Temple in the cloud? ______________________

Acts 2:20a - "....The sun will be turned to DARKNESS...."

Luke 23:44f - On what recent occasion had the sun turned dark? ______________________

Acts 2:20b - "....and the moon to BLOOD before the coming of the great and glorious day of the Lord...."

Luke 23:44f - Whose blood had been spilled recently while it was dark and the moon could be seen?

____

Acts 2:21 - "....And everyone who calls on the name of the Lord will be saved."

Hebrews 10:11 - In the Old Testament era, did animal sacrifices save them? _____________

Hebrews 10:10 - Who had to be sacrificed so we could be saved by him? _____________ Acts 2:1, 38 - When did this privilege begin? _________

Acts 22:16 - What act is included in "calling on his name"? _______________________

2 Thessalonians 2:8-10 - Those representing Satan perform what kinds of miracles, signs and wonders? ____________________________ Will it deceive God's people? _____________

Matthew 7:22-24 - Jesus said on the Day of Judgment, many will declare they prophesied in his name, drove out ________________, and performed many ________________, but Jesus will tell them, "I _________________ knew you. Away from me, you __________________." Jesus wants us to put what into practice? ______________________________

Hebrews 2:4 - By the time Hebrews was written, most of the New Testament had been written down. In this passage, is distribution of signs, wonders and various miracles, and gifts of the Holy Spirit mentioned in the present or past tense? _________________

Miracles In First Century

Quote from Eusebius' Ecclesiastical History, Chapter. VII

"These accounts are given by Irenaeus in those five books of his, to which he gave the title of 'Refutation and Overthrow of False Doctrine.' In the second book of the same work, he also shows that EVEN DOWN TO HIS TIMES [he lived 130-200

AD] instances of divine and MIRACULOUS power were REMAINING IN SOME CHURCHES.

"So far are they from raising the dead, as the Lord raised, and as the apostles by means of prayer, for even among the brethren frequently in a case of necessity when a whole church united in much fasting and prayer, the spirit has returned to the ex-animated body, and the man was granted to the prayers of the saints....

"Some, indeed, most certainly and truly cast out demons, so that frequently those persons themselves that were cleansed from wicked spirits believed and were received into the church.....

"Others have the knowledge of things to come, as also visions and prophetic communications; others heal the sick by the imposition of hands, and restore them to health. And, moreover, as we said above, even the dead have been raised and continued with us many years....

"As we hear, many of the brethren in the church who have prophetic gifts, and who speak in all tongues through the spirit, and who also bring to light the secret things of men for their benefit, and who expound the mysteries of God."

"These gifts of different kinds also continued with those that were worthy until the times mentioned."

What Is Baptism Of The Holy Spirit & Fire?

Matthew 20:22 "You don't know what you are asking," Jesus said to them. "Can you drink the cup I am going to drink?"

Mark 10:38f "You don't know what you are asking," Jesus said. "Can you drink the cup I drink or be baptized with the baptism I am baptized with?" "We can," they answered. Jesus said to them, "You will drink the cup I drink and be baptized with the baptism I am baptized with."

Luke 12:59f "I have come to bring fire on the earth, and how I wish it were already kindled! But I have a baptism to undergo, and how distressed I am until it is completed!"

What Does "Fire" Mean?

I Cor. 3:13 It will be revealed with fire, and the fire will test the quality of each man's work.

I Peter 1:7 These have come so that your faith - of greater worth than gold, which perishes even though refined by fire - may be proved genuine and may result in praise, glory and honor when Jesus Christ is revealed.

Matthew 3:11 [Referred to Pharisees and Sadducees as "You brood of vipers" in v. 7.]

Luke 3:16 "I baptized you with water for repentance. But after me will come one who is more powerful than I....He will baptized you with the Holy Spirit and with fire. His winnowing fork is in his hand...burning up the chaff with unquenchable fire."

If fire is immersion in tests of loyalty to God, could these evil "church" leaders be immersed by the Holy Spirit? _________

John 14:16 Jesus refers to "The Spirit of Truth."

John 17:17 Jesus says "Your [God's] word is truth."

Therefore, these hypocritical church leaders will be baptized by fire of testing and the Word of God. The result will be casting into the unquenchable fire of hell.

Acts 1:5 Half this phrase is carried over to be applied to the Apostles (Acts 1:3). Baptism of fire is conspicuously absent when applied to the Apostles.

"Do not leave Jerusalem, but wait for the gift my Father promised, which you have heard me speak about. For John baptized with water, but in a few days you will be baptized with the Holy Spirit."

Acts 1:8 "You will receive power when the Holy Spirit comes on you."

Acts 1:11 "Men of Galilee," they [angels] said, "why do you stand here looking into the sky?"

Another indication the promise was just to the apostles, men of Galilee.

Acts 1:15 In those days of waiting, they selected a replacement for Judas among how many assembled? ____________________ Verse 14 indicates there were both men and ________________________ present.

Acts 2:1a "When the ____________________ of Pentecost ____________________ ...." Does this indicate the same day as selecting Judas' replacement or another day? ____________________

Acts 2:1b "...they were all together in one place." Who is "they"?

verse 7: Men or women? ___________________
From where? ______________________

verse14: How many stood up together? ________

verse 15: Men or women? ___________________

Acts 2:4a They were ____________________ with the Holy Spirit. The same word is used in Luke 8:23 where the boat they were in was sinking into the water. They were filled because they were being immersed.

Acts 2:4b They began to speak in "tongues." According to verses 6 & 8, were they unknown tongues or recognizable languages? ____________________________________

The Only Other Instance of Baptism of Holy Spirit

Acts 10:44-48a "While Peter was still speaking these words, the Holy Spirit came on _________ who heard the message. The circumcised believers [Jewish Christians] who had come with Peter were ASTONISHED that the gift of the Holy Spirit had been poured out EVEN ON the ____________. For they heard [Greek, understood] them speaking in tongues and praising God. Then Peter said, 'Can anyone keep these people from being baptized with ____________________? They have received the Holy Spirit just as we have.' So he _______________________ that they be baptized in the name of Jesus."

Question: When Peter said, "They have received the Holy Spirit just as we have," who did he mean by we? He explained it when he reported to the church in Jerusalem.

Acts 11:15 "As I began to speak, the Holy Spirit came on them as he had come on US AT THE BEGINNING."

> What beginning? The Holy Spirit did not come at the beginning of John the Baptist's ministry. The Holy Spirit did not come at the beginning of Jesus' ministry. It did come at the beginning of the church, as noted above.

Acts 2:7 says explains the men who received Holy Spirit were men of ________________ and they were talking to Godfearing ___________________________.

> So the Holy Spirit came on the apostles as representatives of the first Jews in the church at Pentecost, and it came on Cornelius' household as representatives of the first Gentiles in the church.

The Ephesians

Acts 19:2 Did these Ephesians know there was even a Holy Spirit? ________

Acts 19:3-4 They'd been baptized into John's baptism of _____________________.

Acts 19:5 Then, rather than baptize in the name of the Father, Son and Holy Spirit, since they never heard of a Holy Spirit, Paul baptized them into the name of the ___________________ ____________________________.

Acts 19:6 Then to prove to them there was a Holy Spirit, he placed his hands on them afterwards.

In Acts 10:45, the Holy Spirit had been _________________ out. But this time the Holy Spirit _____________________ on them.

Who Had Power to Give Holy Spirit
Apart from Water Baptism?

Acts 2:38 "Peter replied, 'Repent and be baptized, every one of you in the name of Jesus Christ for the forgiveness of your sins. And you WILL receive the gift of the Holy Spirit."

Who Did Cain Marry?

Genesis 4:17 - Cain lay with his _______________ and she became pregnant.

Genesis 5:4 - Adam...had other sons and ____________
(Incest was not a sin until the Law of Moses - Leviticus 18:10.)

What Kind Of Music?

Encyclopedia Britannica Dictionary: "MUSIC. The science and art of the rhythmic combination of tones, VOCAL OR INSTRUMENTAL, embracing melody and harmony."

Old Testament

About 1000 BC (1500 years after Moses gave the Law), David divided up the priests by duties since there were hundreds of them by this time. With God's guidance, he also began additional forms of worship for when the Temple, a permanent stone structure, was built to replace the tabernacle (tent of worship).

1 Chronicles:

6:31f The musicians ministered with music in front of the tabernacle, the Tent of Meeting, until Solomon built the temple of the Lord in Jerusalem. They performed their duties ccording to the ______________________________ laid down for them.

6:33, 38-39 Heman, the musician, was a Kohathite and grandson of what great judge of Israel? __________________ His clan was of Kohath, the son of Levi.

6:39, 42 At Heman's right hand was ________________. His clan was of Gershon, the son of Levi.

6:44, 46 At Heman's left hand was E__________________. His clan was of Merari, the son of Levi.

15:5 How many musicians were in the clan of

Kohath? ____________________

15:6 How many musicians were in the clan of Merari? ____________________

15:7 How many musicians were in the clan of Gershon? __________________

15:16 David told the Levites to appoint (ordain) musicians among them as __________________, accompanied by musical ______________________. Besides these two categories of music, are there any others? _______________

15:17 What three men did the Levites appoint (ordain)? ____ ____

15:19 What instrument were Heman, Asaph and Ethan to play? ____

15:20 What instrument were the next relatives to play? ______________________________

15:21 What instrument were the next men to play? ______________________________

15:22, 27 Who was the choir director? _________________ _________________________________

16:4 David appointed some of the Levites to do what four things?
(1) Minister before the ____________________,
(2) make ___________________________________,
(3) give thanks, and
(4) praise ____________________________.

16:5 Asaph, the orchestra leader, was to sound the ______________________________ [set the tempo] and the others were to play the ______________________________ and ______________________________.

16:6 Regularly two other men were to blow the ______________________________ before the ark.

16:7 Who supplied them with their first song of praise? ______________________________

16:37 This orchestra ministered before the ark regularly, every ________________ as required.

If we adopt this Old Testament regulation, what must we have in the church building every day? ____
____
____

16:42 Heman and Jeduthun were responsible for sounding the ____________________________________ and ________________________________ and for playing the other ______________________________________.

23:5 How many, if they all performed at once, were in the Temple orchestra? ______________________

23:30 The musicians were required to stand every __________________________ to thank and praise the Lord. they were to do the same every __________________

23:31 Furthermore, they were to perform whenever _______________________________________ were presented on Sabbaths and at New Moon festivals and at appointed feasts. They were to serve before the Lord _________________________________ and in the proper ____ and in the way _______________________________________ for them.

25:1 Many years after David brought the ark to Jerusalem and when he was about to die, he determined the following would serve as musicians in the temple:______________

____

____________ (apparently Ethan had died by this time).

They were to prophesy in song, accompanied by what three specified instruments? ______________________________

____

____

25:6 The music of the temple was required to include what three instruments? ____________________________________

____.

25:7 How many of the 4000 musicians noted above were trained and skilled in music? ____________________

2 Chronicles

5:13 When the temple was completed under David's son, Solomon, and the Ark of the Covenant delivered to the Temple, the Levites praised God with full orchestra and chorus. They were dressed in fine ______________________ and played what three instruments? _____________________

____

Did they sing in harmony or unison? ________________

God showed his approval when the ____________________________________ of the Lord _____________________ the temple.

29:25 Whose command were they following by playing these four instruments in the Temple worship? __________________

New Testament Comparisons

Hebrews 7:22 In the Christian era we have a _________________________ covenant.

Hebrews 8:13 By calling this covenant "new," Jesus has made the first one ________________________.

Hebrews 10:1 That old law was only a ______________ of the good things that are coming - not the ____________ themselves.

> Leviticus 21:1,10,21 In the O.T., high priests were appointed (anointed/ordained) from among the priests, the descendants of who? ____________________

Hebrews 7:24-26 Jesus has become our permanent high ________________________.

> Lev. 23:26; 16:2,17 How often did the Day of Atonement occur? ____________________ How often could the high priest enter the Most Holy Place? ____________________

Hebrews 9:11, 24 Where is the Most Holy Place under the Christian testament? ____________________

> Lev. 16:6f, 24 What did the high priest sacrifice under the old testament? ____________________

Hebrews 10:4, 10 Who was sacrificed under the new testament? ____________________________ He was also called what (John 1:35)? _____________________________

> 1 Chron. 15:3, 16:1 Where was the tabernacle (tent of worship) under King David? ____________________

> 2 Chron. 3:1 Where was the permanent temple under King Solomon? _________________________

Hebrews 9:11 Where is the tabernacle/temple under the new testament? ________________________

Exodus 26:31f What was behind the curtain under the old testament? __________________

Hebrews 10:20 Who became the curtain under the new testament? ___________________

Lev. 16:14 What was the high priest to sprinkle the blood on under the old testament? ______________________________

Hebrews 10:22 What is the blood sprinkled on under the new testament? ____________________________

Exodus 30:7 Incense was offered which times of the day under the old testament? _______________

Revelation 8:4 What is the incense under the new testament? _______________________

What about worship? Hebrews 13:14 says the music part of our worship is to offer to God our sacrifice of praise -- the fruit of our lips. The service is led by priests and all Christians are priests (1 Peter 2:5). Romans 12:1 says we are to offer our bodies as daily sacrifices instead of the daily sacrifices offered in the Temple.

If we decide to keep part of the Old Testament forms of worship, we must keep them all. James 2:10 says, "Whoever keeps the ____________________ law, yet stumbles at just ________________ point, is guilty of breaking _______________ of it." Thus, if we revert to O.T. forms of worship, it must also include animal sacrifices, etc. Colossians 2:14 says God nailed all these written laws to the cross with our sins.

EPHESIANS 5:19 tells us how to sing and what kind of instrument we are to accompany our singing with: "SPEAK to one another with psalms, hymns and spiritual songs. SING and MAKE MUSIC IN YOUR HEART to the Lord. In the original Greek, the word "melody" is "psallo" which means a stringed instrument. This scripture is telling us to play on the instrument of our heart.

God was specific when he designated singers and players in the Old Testament. Did he forget something when he made his designations in the New Testament? He specified sing in these verses: Romans 15:9, 1 Corinthians 14:15, Ephesians 5:19, Colossians 3:16, Hebrews 2:12, James 5:13. He never specified which instruments to play, something he always did previously. Examples of music in the early church and with Jesus himself always say sing, but never say play: Matthew 26:30, Mark 14:26, Acts 16:25

The only playing mentioned in the New Testament is in heaven where is also located the altar of incense and other furnishings of the Temple. All of this, Hebrews explains, is symbolic of the higher spiritual level of worship.

Some may say that the singing sounds better with an instrument. Using that same logic, we could say the Lord's Supper would taste better if we had lemon pie instead of unleavened bread. Who are we worshipping? Ourselves or God? Who are we trying to please? Ourselves or God? Who made the rules? Ourselves or God? Colossians 2:8 and 23 warns of self-will worship.

Why would we want to be satisfied with the material, when we can have the spiritual on a higher plane, as explained in Hebrews 10:1. The material things are not reality; things on the spiritual level are reality.

Dancing To The Lord

Old Testament References

Exodus 15:20f - Then Miriam the prophetess, Aaron's sister, took a tambourine in her hand, and all the women followed her, with tambourines and dancing. Miriam sang to them: "Sing to the Lord, for he is highly exalted."

2 Samuel 6:16 - As the ark of the Lord was entering the City of David....King David leaping and dancing before the Lord.

1 Chronicles 15:29 - As the ark of the covenant of the Lord was entering the City of David....King David dancing and celebrating.

Psalm 30:11f - You turned my wailing into dancing; you removed my sackcloth and clothed me with joy, that my heart may sing to you and not be silent. O Lord my God, I will give you thanks forever.

Psalm 149:3 - Let them praise his name with dancing and make music to him with tambourine and harp.

Psalm 150:3f - Praise him with the sounding of the trumpet, praise him with the harp and lyre, praise him with tambourine and dancing, praise him with the strings and flute, praise him with the clash of cymbals, praise him with resounding cymbals.

CONCLUSION: Singing and dancing were worship

New Testament References

Matthew 11:16f - To what can I compare this generation? They are like CHILDREN sitting in the MARKETPLACES and calling out to others: "We played the flute for you and you did not dance; we sang a dirge and you did not mourn."

Matthew 14:6 - On Herod's birthday the daughter of Herodias danced for them and pleased Herod so much.

Mark 6:22 - When the daughter of Herodias came in and danced, she pleased Herod and his dinner guests.

Luke 7:32 - They are like children sitting in the marketplace and calling out to each other: "We played the flute for you and you did not dance; we sang a dirge and you did not cry.

Luke 15:25f - Meanwhile the older son was in the field. When he came near the house, he heard music and dancing....Your has come and your father has killed the fatted calf.

CONCLUSION: Singing and dancing were never worship.

Doesn't God Choose Me,
I Don't Choose God?

Predestined/Elected for salvation.
Everyone else has to go to hell.

Below are all the verses regarding Christians which use the word choose, chosen, called, predestined, elected.

These verses using "choose," "elect" or "called" come from the same Greek word ***kletos,*** and variations such as ***kaleo***, and ***klesis,*** meaning to INVITE, not choose.

Romans 1:1, 6, 7; 8:28, 30; 9:11, 24f; 11:29
1 Corinthians 1:1, 2, 9, 24, 26; 7:15, 17, 18, 20, 21, 22, 24
Galatians 1:6, 15; 5:8, 13
Ephesians 1:18; 4:1, 4, 14
Philippians 3:14
Colossians 3:15
1 Thessalonians 2:12; 5:24
2 Thessalonians 1:11; 2:14
1 Timothy 6:12
2 Timothy 1:9
Hebrews 3:1; 5:4; 9:15; 11:8, 18
1 Peter 1:15; 2:21; 3:9; 5:10
2 Peter 1:3, 10
Jude 1
Revelation 17:14; 19:9, 11, 13

These verses using "elect" or "predestined" come from the same Greek word ***eklektos*** and variations such as ***ekloge***, and means to CALL out. These same passages also contain the word INVITE, as you can see from the above:

Romans 8:33; 9:11; 11:5, 7, 28;
Ephesians 1:4
Colossians 3:12

1 Peter 1:2; 2:4, 6, 9; 5:13
2 Peter 1:10
Revelation 17:14

The following verse uses the word ***haireomai*** meaning to lift up for oneself, to take:

2 Thessalonians 2:13

The only verses using "choose" or variations with no close proximity to "invite" passages are these:

Romans 16:13 - a particular brother, Rufus
1 Thessalonians 1:4 - chosen because gospel came to them
2 Timothy 2:19 - chosen must turn away from wickedness
Titus 1:1 - knowledge of truth & faith led to hope of eternal life
James 2:7 - belong to God

The following verses have the word ***epikaleo*** in it telling sinners to "call" on God requesting salvation.

Acts 2:21 - "_________________________ who calls on the name of the Lord will be saved."

Acts 22:16 - "And now, what are you ____________for? Get up, be ______________________ and __________________ your sins away, _____________________ on his name.

Romans 10:13-14 - "_____________________ who calls on the name of the Lord will be _______________. How, then, can they call on the one they have not believed in?"

1 Corinthians 1:2 - "To the church of God...together with _____ those ______________________ who call on the name of our Lord.

1 Peter 1:17 - "Since you call on a Father who judges _________ man's work __________________________."
Below are verses that show that salvation is offered to

everyone

Mark 16:15 - "Go into ____________ the world and preach the good new to ____________ creation. _____________________ believes and is baptized will be saved.

John 3:16 - "For God so loved the ____________________ that he gave his one and only Son, that ______________________ believes in him shall not perish but have eternal life."

John 3:36 - "_____________________ believes in the Son has eternal life, but whoever ____________________ the son will not see life."

1 Timothy 2:4 - "God...wants ______________________ to be saved."

2 Peter 3:9b - "God...is patient with you,___________________ ____ to perish, but _____________________ to come to repentance."

Aren't Christians Egotistical And Intolerant To Claim Their Religion Is The Only Way To Heaven?

We must read the "scriptures" of other world religions and try to prove their divinity.

The only "scriptures" that can be proven by external evidences (prophecies of nations come true, scientific facts, etc.) is the Bible.

By the same token, it is not egotistical and intolerant to say that penicillin is the only cure for certain diseases.

Thank You

Thanks for reading my book! I'm so honored that you chose to spend your precious time with my research. You are appreciated. I'm an author who relies on my readers to help spread the word about stories you enjoy and facts you discover. Would you take a few minutes to let your friends know on Facebook, Pinterest... wherever you go online?

Also, each honest review on bookseller websites means a lot to me and helps other readers know if this is a book they might enjoy.

About The Author

Katheryn Maddox Haddad grew up in northern USA and now lives in India, where she doesn't have to shovel sunshine. She basks in 100-degree weather with banana trees, monkeys, and a computer with most of the letters worn off.

Besides the US and India, she has lived in four other countries ~ Korea, Canada, Afghanistan, and Abu Dhabi, and has made short visits to Tokyo and Sri Lanka.

With a bachelor's degree in English, Bible, and social science from Harding University and part of a master's degree in Bible from the Harding Graduate School of Theology (including Greek), she also has a master's degree in human relations from Abilene Christian University.

She spends half her day writing and the other half teaching English over the internet worldwide using the Bible as a textbook. She has taught nearly 10,000 Muslims over 15 years in the Middle East. Students she has converted to Christianity are in hiding in Afghanistan, Iran, Iraq, Yemen, Jordan, Uzbekistan, Tajikistan, and Palestine. "They are my heroes," she declares.

Currently, she also teaches Bible history at the MH School of Theology in Punadipadu, Krishna, Andhra Pradesh, India.

She is a member of American Christian Fiction Writers, the American Historical Association, World History Association, World Archaeological College, Association of Ancient Historians, and Archaeological Research Institute.

Oh, and for her next birthday, she plans to ride an elephant.

Connect With the Author

FACEBOOK

I welcome contact from readers, which you can do here:

Pictorial INDEX to all books & categories
Website: https://NorthernLightsPublishingHouse.com
Come read a sample chapter of each book

Facebook JUST ME Profile:
https://www.facebook.com/ReadsForAllAges/
Daily inspiration, poster, & prayer

Facebook BOOKS Page
https://www.facebook.com/katheryn.maddox.haddad/
Get in on weekly discounts only known by you

PINTEREST
https://www.pinterest.com/haddad1940/

YOUTUBE
https://www.youtube.com/@KH-bi3fr

email: khaddad1940@gmail.com

Buy Your Next Book Now

BIBLICAL HISTORICAL NOVELS
Series of 8: Soul Journey With the Real Jesus
Ongoing Series of 8: Intrepid Men of God

CHILDREN'S BIBLE STORYBOOKS
Series of 8: A Child's Life of Christ
Series of 10: A Child's Bible Heroes
Series of 8: A Child's Bible Kids

WORLDWIDE HISTORICAL RESEARCH
DOCUMENTARY, THESIS, NOVEL & SCREENPLAY WRITERS

BIBLE TOPICS
Applied Christianity: Handbook 500 Good Works
Christianity or Islam? The Contrast
The Holy Spirit: 592 Verses Examined
Inside the Hearts of Bible Women-Reader+Audio+Leader
Revelation: A Love Letter From God
Worship Changes Since 1st Century + Worship 1st Century Way
Was Jesus God? (Why Evil)
365 Life-Changing Scriptures Day by Date
The Road to Heaven
The Lord's Supper: 52 Readings with Prayers

BIBLE FUN BOOKS
Bible Puzzles, Bible Song Book, Bible Numbers

TOUCHING GOD SERIES
365 Golden Bible Thoughts: God's Heart to Yours
365 Pearls of Wisdom: God's Soul to Yours
365 Silver-Winged Prayers: Your Spirit to God's

SURVEY SERIES: EASY BIBLE WORKBOOKS
→Old Testament & New Testament Surveys
→Questions You Have Asked-Part I & II

Genealogy: How to Climb Your Family Tree Without Falling Out
Volume I & 2: Beginner-Intermediate & Colonial-Medieval

Genealogy: How to Climb Your Family Tree Without Falling Out
Volume I & 2: Beginner-Intermediate & Colonial-Medieval

www.ingramcontent.com/pod-product-compliance
Lightning Source LLC
Chambersburg PA
CBHW060421050426
42449CB00009B/2058
9781952261510